Awake! Speak Life 21 Day Devotional:
Let's Be Intentional About Our Happiness.

Nichole Shirell

Nichole Shirell Enterprises
Pensacola, Florida

Awake! Speak Life 21 Day Devotional: Let's Be Intentional About Our Happiness.

Copyright © 2018 Nichole Shirell

Published by Nichole Shirell Enterprises
9091 Airway Dr. #924
Pensacola Fl 32514

All rights reserved. No part of this publication may be reproduced, stored in a retrieval system, or transmitted in any form by any means – electronic, mechanical, photocopy, recording, scanning, or otherwise – except for brief quotations in critical reviews or articles, without the prior written permission of the publisher, and except as provided by USA copyright law.

Cover design: Nichole Shirell
Cover Image: Pixabay https://pixabay.com/en/rain-lily-zephyranthes-grandiflora-3152766/
Editor: Tonya Phillips
First Printing 2018
Printed in the United States of America

Choose life! For the next 21 days use the techniques found in "Awake! Speak Life 21 Day Devotional" to strategically change your focus and receive God's gift of abundance by intentionally speaking change into being.

This book is not a substitute for medical advice from a physician. The reader should regularly consult a physician as necessary.

Scripture references are from The Holy Bible.

All rights reserved.

ISBN-13: 978-1985896895
ISBN-10: 1985896893

AWAKE!

DEDICATION

All honor and glory to God! I am who I am because of my desire to serve Him. I pray that all who read are blessed.

Table of Contents

Introduction vii

1 God's Love 1

2 Closer to God 9

3 Intecessory Prayer 15

4 Discouragement / Encouragement 26

5 Focus 34

6 Disobedience / Obedience 42

7 Trust God 50

ABOUT THE AUTHOR 56

Introduction

The contents of AWAKE! are divided into seven chapters. Each chapter breaks down all lessons into three sections. It is the expectation that readers will participate daily over a three-week time frame. The author's purpose is increase knowledge by requiring written, verbal and memorization of affirmations and scriptures.

1 God's Love

Day One:

"You do not have to accept everything!" said my mother reassuringly in her subtly way of reminding me that I am not garbage. I am the prize. But most importantly, God is the only continuous, constant, and consistent love of which I can depend.

Assignment:

1. Read Deuteronomy 31:1-6:

    a. Make a note every time you find the following "The LORD will" statement in the scripture.

Nichole Shirell

2. Read Hebrews 13:1-6:

   a. Make a note of written guidance from Paul which details the actions we should strive to achieve and also avoid.

Notes:

AWAKE!

Day Two:

Assignment One:

1. Read and memorize the following scriptures:

Old Testament: Deuteronomy 31:6 NIV

- "Be strong and courageous. Do not be afraid or terrified because of them, for the LORD your God goes with; he will never leave you nor forsake you."

New Testament: Hebrews 13:5 NIV

- "Keep your lives free from the love of money and be content with what you have, because God has said, "Never will I leave you; never will I forsake you."

Nichole Shirell

Notes:

Day Three

Assignment:

1. Today look in the mirror.
2. Recite Deuteronomy 31:1-6 NIV and Hebrews 13:5 NIV.
3. Read the affirmation statements below.
4. Repeat to yourself 3 times.

Affirmation:

- God loves me! He cares! No matter who leaves, he will not leave.
- God loves me! And, I love myself.

Nichole Shirell

Notes:

Day Four:

Assignment:

1. Recite Deuteronomy 31:1-6 NIV and Hebrews 13:5 NIV.
2. Write two things in the space below which is a self-commitment or a task that you can add today. Remember the two things are examples that you 1. know God loves you and 2. love yourself.

Focus and Awareness:
- Today I will:
1. Read affirmation statements in the mirror out loud.

2. Smile today, all day.

3.

4.

Notes:

2 Closer to God

DAY FIVE:

There are some situations that require us to draw closer to God who is a cure for every ailment, issue, or burden.

We should withdraw from the world and seek Jesus when the load becomes heavy. You may ask: how can I get closer? What can I do? My answer is prayer.

Assignment:

1. Read and memorize the following scriptures: Old Testament: Psalm 73:28 NIV:

- "But as for me, it is good to be near God. I

have made the Sovereign LORD my refuge; I will tell of all your deeds."

New Testament: James 4:8 NIV:

- "Come near to God and he will come near to you. Wash your hands, you sinners, and purify your hearts, you doubled-minded."

Notes:

Day Six:

Assignment:

1. Look in a mirror and recite Psalm 73:28 NIV and James 4:8 NIV.
2. Read the affirmation statements listed below in a mirror.
3. Repeat 3 times.

Affirmation:

- "Is anyone among you in trouble? Let them pray. Is anyone happy? Let them sing songs of praise." James 5:13 NIV
- When I am happy, I will praise.
- When I am sad, I will give pray.

Nichole Shirell

Notes:

Day Seven:

Assignment:

1. Look in a mirror and recite Psalm 73:28 NIV and James 4:8 NIV.
2. Read day six affirmation statements in a mirror to yourself out loud.
3. Repeat 3 times.
4. Write two things in the space below which is a self-commitment that you can add today. Remember the two things are examples of how you will draw closer to God.

Focus and Awareness:

- Today I will...

1. Read affirmation statements in the mirror out loud.
2. Read scripture.
3.
4.

Notes:

3 Intecessory Prayer

Day Eight

I am a firm believer that I am alive today because of my Mother and Grandmother praying for me.

There are many examples of people praying for others in the bible. Two excellent examples are: first, Abraham's conversation with God before the destruction of Sodom found in Genesis 18:16-33; and secondly, Jesus's prayer for all believers which is detailed in John 17:20-23.

Nichole Shirell

Assignment:

1. Read and memorize the following scriptures:

Old Testament:

- Deuteronomy 9:18-19 NIV:
    - "Then once again I fell prostrate before the LORD for forty days and forty nights; I ate no bread and drank no water, because of all the sin you had committed, doing what was evil in the LORD's sight and so

arousing his anger. I feared the anger and wrath of the LORD, for he was angry enough with you to destroy you. But again the LORD listened to me."

- Exodus 34:9 NIV:
  - "Lord," he said, "if I have found favor in your eyes, then let the Lord go with us. Although this is a stiff-necked people, forgive our wickedness and our sin, and

Nichole Shirell

take us as your inheritance."

AWAKE!

Day Nine

Assignment:

1. Read and memorize the following scriptures:

New Testament

- Matthew 5:44 NIV:
    - "But I tell you, love your enemies and pray for those who persecute you."
- Ephesians 6:18 NIV:

Nichole Shirell

- "And pray in the Spirit on all occasions with all kinds of prayers and requests. With this in mind, be alert and always keep on praying for all the Lord's people."

Notes

Day Ten

Assignment:

1. Look in a mirror and recite one of the following scriptures: Deuteronomy 9:18-19 NIV or Exodus 34:9 NIV.

2. Look in a mirror and recite one of the following scriptures: Matthew 5:44 NIV or Ephesians 6:18 NIV

3. Read the affirmation statement below in a mirror.

4. Repeat 3 times.

Affirmation:

- God loves and cares for me and I will talk to him instead of man.

Notes:

Day Eleven

Assignment:

1. Look in a mirror and recite one of the following scriptures: Deuteronomy 9:18-19 NIV or Exodus 34:9 NIV.
2. Look in a mirror and recite one of the following scriptures: Matthew 5:44 NIV or Ephesians 6:18 NIV
3. Read the affirmation statements from day ten in a mirror out loud.

4. Repeat 3 times.

5. Write four things in the space provided below which is a self-commitment that you can do today. Remember the two things are examples of your commitment to improve your prayer life.

Focus and Awareness:

- Today I will...

1.

2.

3.

AWAKE!

4.

Notes:

Nichole Shirell

4 Discouragement / Encouragement
Day Twelve

What is that one thing / talent certain individuals speak negatively about? Some may use your talent against you. Or, some may continuously remind you of a past way of life from which you are now free. When constructive criticism condemns, it is in actuality destructive censorship. And, when conversation reminds you of your past, remember you are a new creature in Christ, forgiven and free.

I challenge you, continue to sow into your gift. Remember, the enemy will use the people that are the closest to you to cause you to doubt. During this time, you must stand the strongest in your faith. Do not give up!

Assignment:

1. Read and memorize the following scripture:

Old Testament: Jeremiah 29:11 KJV:

- "For I know the thoughts that I think

toward you, saith the LORD, thoughts of peace, and not evil, to give you an expected end."

New Testament: Hebrews 11:6 KJV:

- "But without faith it is impossible to please him: for he that cometh to God must believe that he is, and that he is a rewarder of those that diligently seek him."

Notes:

Day Thirteen

Assignment:

1. Look in a mirror and recite both of the following scriptures: Jeremiah 29:11 KJV and Hebrews 11:6 NIV.
2. Read the following affirmation statements in a mirror out loud.
3. Repeat 3 times.

Affirmation:

- I am who the Word says I am.

- I can do what the Word says I can do.
- I will encourage myself.

Notes:

Day Fourteen

Assignment:

1. Look in a mirror and recite both of the following scriptures: Jeremiah 29:11 KJV and Hebrews 11:6 NIV.
2. Read the following affirmation statements in a mirror out loud.
3. Repeat 3 times.

Affirmations:

- I am who the Word says I am.

- I can do what the Word says I can do.
- I will encourage myself.

4. Write four things in the space provided below (commitment to yourself) that you can do today. Remember the two things are examples of your commitment to remove negativity from your life.

Focus and Awareness:

- Today I will...

1.

2.

AWAKE!

3.

4.

Notes:

5 Focus

Day Fifteen

What price are you paying for your inability to move forward? Jesus has to power to break every chain and move every mountain. The longing for the things of the past cost Lot's wife her life. To be free we must turn everything over to God. Follow Jesus! Are you missing your destiny because you are stuck?

Assignment:

1. Read and memorize the following

scriptures:

Old Testament: Jeremiah 1:7-8 NIV:

- "But the LORD said to me, "Do not say, 'I am too young.' You must go to everyone I send you to and say whatever I command you. ⁸ Do not be afraid of them, for I am with you and will rescue you," declares the LORD."

New Testament Matthew 6:33 KJV:

- "But seek ye first the kingdom of God, and his righteousness; and all these

Nichole Shirell

things shall be added unto you."

Notes:

Day Sixteen

Assignment:

1. Look in a mirror and recite both of the following scriptures: Jeremiah 1:7-8 NIV and Matthew 6:33 NIV.
2. Read the following affirmation statement in a mirror out loud.
3. Repeat 3 times.

Affirmation:

- I am not afraid.

Nichole Shirell

- With God all things are possible.

Notes:

AWAKE!

Day Seventeen

Assignment:

- Look in a mirror and recite both of the following scriptures: Jeremiah 1:7-8 NIV and Matthew 6:33 11:6 NIV.

- Read the affirmation statements from day sixteen in a mirror out loud.

- Repeat 3 times.

- Write four things in the space below (commitment to yourself) that you can do today. Remember these are examples of your commitment to focus on the future.

Focus and Awareness:

- Today I will...

1.

2.

3.

4.

AWAKE!

Notes:

Nichole Shirell

6 Disobedience / Obedience
Day Eighteen

When your steps are ordered by God and you decide to run away, you are running in place!

This reminds me of the story of Jonah. There were times in my own life when I wanted desperately to just do me. However, living in the world is not my destiny. The world causes an immeasurable amount of pain. Do I know where the road leads? No, but, what I do know is that because I am striving to be an obedient child of God, the turbulence of this world does not affect me as it once did.

Assignment One:

1. Read and take notes from the following scriptures:

Old Testament: Read the book of Jonah: chapters 1 and 2.

- Jonah 1:1-17
- Jonah 2:1-10

New Testament: John 21:15 – 17 NIV

- "When they had finished eating, Jesus

Nichole Shirell

said to Simon Peter, "Simon son of John, do you love me more than these?" "Yes, Lord," he said, "you know that I love you." Jesus said, "Feed my lambs. Again Jesus said, "Simon son of John, do you love me?" He answered, "Yes, Lord, you know that I love you." Jesus said, "Take care of my sheep. The third time he said to him, "Simon son of John, do you love me?" Peter was hurt because Jesus asked him the third time, "Do you love me?" He said,

"Lord, you know all things; you know that I love you." Jesus said, "Feed my sheep."

Assignment Two:

1. What are three lessons that are evident from each scripture? List them below.

      a.

      b.

      c.

Nichole Shirell

Notes:

Assignment:

1. Read the following affirmation statements in a mirror out loud.
2. Repeat 3 times.

Affirmation:

- I am not of the world. I am of a royal priesthood.
- I am not afraid.
- With God all things are possible.

Nichole Shirell

Day Nineteen

Assignment:

1. Read the affirmation statements from day nineteen in a mirror out loud.
2. Repeat 3 times.
3. Write four things in the space provided below (commitment to yourself) that you can do today. Remember the four things are examples of your commitment to align your will with God's will.

AWAKE!

Focus and Awareness:

- Today I will...

  1.

  2.

  3.

  4.

Notes:

7 Trust God

Day Twenty

It is because of our faith that we receive. Our faith is equivalent to our belief. Our belief is equivalent to our ability to trust God.

Assignment One:

1. Read and memorize the following scriptures:

Old Testament: Proverbs 3:5-6

- "Trust in the LORD with all your heart and lean not on your own understanding; in all your ways submit to him, and he will make your paths straight." NIV

New Testament: Read Hebrews chapter 11. NIV

- "Now faith is confidence in what we hope for and assurance about what we do not see." 11: 1 NIV
- Hebrews chapter 11.

Day Twenty-One

Assignment Two:

1. Read the following affirmation statements in a mirror out loud.
2. Repeat 3 times

Affirmation:

- God loves me! He cares! No matter who leaves, he will not leave.

Assignment three:

3. Write four things in the space provided (commitment to yourself) that you can do today. Remember the four things are

examples of your commitment to trust God.

Focus and Awareness:

- Today I will

1.

2.

3.

4.

8 CONCLUSION

From this day forward choose you. We owe it to ourselves to live our best lives, happy, fulfilled and in abundance. My prayer for us is that we continue to pray daily and look into a mirror speaking abundance into our lives. Most importantly, my prayer is not only for our present; but, it is also for our future. Remember, in order to be successful, we must be intentional and make this our new way of life.

I LOVE YOU!

AWAKE!

NOTES:

Nichole Shirell

ABOUT THE AUTHOR

Nichole Shirell is a Christian author born in Birmingham, Alabama. She is the mother of three young men who were all born in Cleveland, Ohio. She now resides in Pensacola, Florida. Her first Christian novel "The Gift: Encouraging Believers to Find Comfort in Christ" was published in December 2017. She is also a contributing poet in the anthology "Unraveling the Layers, Memoirs of a Wounded" published summer 2017. In 2018, her publishing and consulting company Nichole Shirell Enterprises inked their first contract. The company's mission is to simplify the hassle many writers experience when choosing to publish.

For speaking engagements: NicholeShirell@yahoo.com

AWAKE!

Let's Connect:

Communication: NicholeShirell@yahoo.com

Web: nicholeshirell.wixsite.com/nicholeshirell

https://www.facebook.com/IamNicholesf/

https://twitter.com/NicholeShirell

https://www.instagram.com/nichole.shirell/

https://www.pinterest.com/iamNicholesf/

Made in the USA
Columbia, SC
09 May 2018